Economics in Action

How do Mortgages, Loans, and Credit Work?

Jeri Cipriano

Crabtree Publishing Company

www.crabtreebooks.com

Crabtree Publishing Company

www.crabtreebooks.com

Author: Jeri Cipriano
Publishing plan research and development:
   Sean Charlebois, Reagan Miller
   Crabtree Publishing Company
Coordinating editor: Chester Fisher
Series editor: Gare Thompson Associates
Editor: Molly Aloian
Proofreaders: Crystal Sikkens
Editorial Director: Katherine Middleton
Production coordinator: Margaret Salter
Prepress technician: Margaret Salter
Project manager: Kumar Kunal (Q2AMEDIA)
Art direction: Harleen Mehta (Q2AMEDIA)
Cover design: Shruti Aggarwal (Q2AMEDIA)
Design: Jasmeen Kaur, Shruti Aggarwal (Q2AMEDIA)
Photo research: Debabrata Sen (Q2AMEDIA)

Photographs:
Big Stock Photo: Feverpitch Pro: p. 25
Corbis: Mia Song/Star Ledger: p. 5; Gabe Palmer: p. 9;
   James Leynse: p. 23; Paul Barton: p. 26
Dreamstime: p. 6, 11; Dmitriy Shironosov: p. 10;
   Penelope Berger: p. 15 (bottom)
Fotolia: Eléonore H: p. 7
Istockphoto: Gina Sanders: p. 13; Pawel Gaul: p. 19;
   Justin Horrocks: cover
Photolibrary: Roy Morsch: p. 8, 29
Photostogo: title page, p. 16, 17, 20, 24, 28
Q2AMedia Art Bank : p. 25
Reuters: Ed Harris: p. 4
Shutterstock: p. 14; Arenacreative: p. 12; Kjolak: p. 15 (middle),
   17; Vovan: p. 18; Maksim Toome: p. 21; Marie C. Fields: cover

Library and Archives Canada Cataloguing in Publication

Cipriano, Jeri S.
   How do mortgages, loans, and credit work? / Jeri Cipriano.

(Economics in action)
Includes index.
ISBN 978-0-7787-4445-0 (bound).--ISBN 978-0-7787-4456-6 (pbk.)

   1. Loans--Juvenile literature. 2. Credit--Juvenile literature.
3. Mortgage loans--Juvenile literature. I. Title. II. Series: Economics
in action (St. Catherines, Ont.)

HG3701.C56 2010   j332.7   C2009-906270-4

Library of Congress Cataloging-in-Publication Data

Cipriano, Jeri S.
 How do mortgages, loans, and credit work? / Jeri Cipriano.
   p. cm. -- (Economics in action)
 Includes index.
 ISBN 978-0-7787-4456-6 (pbk. : alk. paper) -- ISBN 978-0-7787-4445-0
(reinforced library binding : alk. paper)
 1. Loans--Juvenile literature. 2. Credit--Juvenile literature. 3. Mortgage
loans--Juvenile literature. I. Title. II. Series.

 HG3701.C57 2010
 332.7--dc22

                                                      2009042776

Crabtree Publishing Company

www.crabtreebooks.com   1-800-387-7650

Printed in the USA/122009/BG20091103

Published in Canada
Crabtree Publishing
616 Welland Ave.
St. Catharines, ON
L2M 5V6

Published in the United States
Crabtree Publishing
PMB 59051
350 Fifth Avenue, 59th Floor
New York, New York 10118

Published in the United Kingdom
Crabtree Publishing
Maritime House
Basin Road North, Hove
BN41 1WR

Published in Australia
Crabtree Publishing
386 Mt. Alexander Rd.
Ascot Vale (Melbourne)
VIC 3032

Contents

Borrowing
and Lending

You know what borrowing and lending are. You've been borrowing and lending for years. You ask to borrow five dollars from a friend until you get your allowance. You lend a sleeping bag to a neighbor for a camping trip.

You continue to borrow as you get older. However, the rules surrounding borrowing get more complicated.

- **Consumers** borrow on **credit** to buy things they need or want, such as clothes, TVs, or computers.

- Businesses use credit to grow and expand.

- Governments use credit to repair roads or finance new programs.

- Countries help one another with credit and **loans**.

Our society revolves around borrowing and lending, as does our **market economy**. A market economy is one that allows the choices people make to determine what is produced and sold. It sets the prices of goods and services according to people's **demand** for them as well as the **supply**, or availability, of these goods and services.

▼ These African women are lending each other money.

▲ It's better to save for a luxury item than to borrow money to buy it.

Why Borrow? And Should You?

At the mall, you wander into one of those hi-tech company stores. The salesperson is saying, "This high def TV comes with stop action. You can freeze the frame and actually see each player's moves in slow motion. It's like being right at the game—only better!"

"Wow!" you think. "My family will want to get that TV right away! Wait until I tell them about it." Your parents probably don't have a lot of money lying around with no plans for how to spend it. So in order to make a big purchase, such as that TV, they would have to borrow money.

Is borrowing in order to buy a luxury item a good idea? There are reasons people borrow—some good; some not so good. You have to decide which is which.

Point of Information

Borrowing and lending happens at all levels. The World Bank, a global organization, lends money to help less–developed nations. These nations might use the money to build schools or provide better health care.

Why do People Borrow Money?

People borrow money for a number of reasons. Some are unavoidable. Some are a choice. It's important to know which is which, so you can make smart decisions about spending.

Reasons for borrowing money can include:

- **Emergencies** In life, unexpected things happen all the time. Your dad's car breaks down. Suddenly, he's faced with a $550 repair bill.

- **Critical needs** Your older sister is getting ready to start college. Your parents need to borrow money to finance her first year.

- **Start-up cash for business** Your mom leaves her staff job to set up her own business from home. She needs a computer system and furniture. To cover start-up expenses, she needs to borrow money now and pay it back once the business gets going.

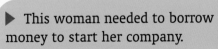
▶ This woman needed to borrow money to start her company.

- **A must-have-now product or service**
  Remember that high def TV? There are people who really want that TV—now! They can't wait until they save up for it.

The last reason is one that should make you stop and think. When you see something you really want, ask yourself:

- *Why do I want this?*
- *Do I really need it?*
- *Do I need it now?*
- *What will I think about it in a couple of months?*
- *Will I like it then as much as I do now?*

Asking questions like these help you spend your money wisely.

▼ Think and ask questions before you buy.

Who's Who and What's What?

With credit, just as with any kind of business exchange, different people play different roles. There are also terms and processes that need to be considered.

◀ You can borrow a CD from a friend.

Who's Involved?

You listen to a friend's CD. You like it and want to buy it, but there's a problem. You don't have enough money to buy it, so you have to borrow money from your sister. She agrees to lend you the money. You are the borrower, she is the lender. The same roles exist at many different levels.

- **Borrower** (individuals, businesses, and countries)

- **Lender** (businesses, banks, governments, friends, and family members)

▲ Sometimes, friends will lend you money to buy things. Then you pay them back.

What's Involved?

If you borrow money from friends or family, you usually just have to pay them back. But when you borrow from a bank or other institution, there's a little more involved. Here are a few terms you should know.

- **Loans** There are different kinds of loans. The most common are personal loans, auto loans, student loans, credit card loans, and mortgages.

- **Debt** When you borrow, your **debt** is the money you owe.

- **Interest** Banks charge interest on every loan they give. The **interest** is added to the amount that is borrowed. So people who get loans pay back more money than they borrowed. This interest is how the bank makes money.

- **Credit** You use credit when you borrow money, usually for a **fee** plus interest. Credit lets you buy now and pay later.

- **Terms** It is important to understand the conditions of your agreement, whether it is for a loan or for a credit card.

So How Does It Work?

A loan is an agreement that involves a borrower and a lender. The lender provides money (or property) to the borrower, who agrees to pay for it over an agreed-upon period of time. The borrower usually agrees to pay back the original sum, plus interest.

Why does this system work? The borrower is able to get funds he or she would not be able to pull together in one lump sum to make a particular purchase. The lender profits from the interest earned.

▲ The lender trusts the borrower to pay back the loan.

▲ The central bank in the United States is the Federal Reserve.

The Hidden Costs: Interest Rates

Interest rates—what you pay in addition to the amount of a loan—are a critical part of almost any loan, but borrowers often don't consider them as carefully as they should.

How are interest rates set? The central bank of the United States is called the Federal Reserve. It is independent from the government, although the U.S. president appoints the bank's president. The Federal Reserve sets the rate at which it lends money to banks. In turn, banks charge interest to their customers over and above the rate the banks have to pay.

Suppose the Federal Reserve charges banks 1 percent to borrow money. If a bank charges you an interest rate of 4.5 percent, it makes a 3.5 percent profit. Another bank may want to attract customers, so it may charge an interest rate of 4 percent. That's why it's important to shop around for the best rate.

Economics in Action

Sometimes, even banks have to borrow money. They may need extra money to meet customers' demands. For example, customers borrow much more heavily around the holiday season. Where do banks get this extra cash? They borrow it from their regional Federal Reserve Bank.

11

Very Interest-ing

Interest rates may vary from institution to institution. There are also differences in the types of interest charged and when interest is paid.

Suppose two people apply for a loan of $10,000. The $10,000 is the principal, the initial amount of money that is lent, to which interest is added. Factors such as the interest rate and the kind of interest charged may result in a different total cost of the loan (principal plus interest) for each individual.

Each time you pay your bill, you're paying part of the **balance** (the amount of the initial loan that still remains after some of the principal has been paid off) plus interest. How often is interest computed? It can vary. It can be monthly, semi-annually, or annually. All this can affect the total cost of a loan.

There are also two main types of interest: **simple interest** and **compound interest**. Simple interest is calculated on the original principal only. It never changes. Usually, simple interest is charged for short-term loans that are repaid within a year or two.

◀ You pay more money on a loan with compound interest.

▲ A loan officer explains how a loan works to borrowers.

Compound interest is calculated on the original sum of money plus the interest that is charged each period. The combined numbers become the new principal for the next pay period. So the amount you pay is always changing and always going up.

If you borrow $10,000 for three years at 5% annual interest compounded annually, this is what you'd pay:

Year	Principal	Interest
Year 1	$10,000 x 5%=	$500
Year 2	($10,000 + $500) x 5%=	$525
Year 3	($10,000 + $500 + $525) x 5%=	$551.25
Total interest:	$500 + $525 + $551.25=	$1,576.25

Compare this to $1,500 interest paid over the same number of years using simple interest!

Suppose you took out a loan for a period of time much longer than three years. How do you think compound interest would compare to simple interest then?

It's in the Cards

One of the most common types of loans is the kind you get through a credit card. In effect, you are borrowing money from the credit card company in order to buy what you need or want.

Who Issues Credit Cards and Why?

Some experts say that credit cards are the banking industry's biggest business. That is, banks make most of their money from the credit cards they issue. Besides banks, many businesses, from gas companies to department stores, offer credit cards.

Credit card companies compete for your business. Some offer frequent flyer miles. Others offer reward points that can be redeemed for merchandise. Some even donate money to your favorite charity with each purchase you make!

Why do credit card companies try to outdo each other with consumer "bonuses?" Once you understand how credit cards work, you'll know why. (Hint: Do these great offers ever keep you from checking out interest rates or penalty fees?)

The Rise of "Plastic Money"

From the 1700s until the early 1900s, European tallymen sold clothing in exchange for small weekly payments. They were called tallymen because they kept a tally, or record, of what people bought. On one side of a wooden stick, they made notches to represent the amount of debt. On the other side, they made notches to keep track of payments.

In 1950, the first plastic money appeared when Diner's Club and American Express came out with charge cards. Then, in 1951, Diner's Club issued the first credit card to 200 customers. These customers could use the card at 27 restaurants in New York City. (Hence the name: Diner's Club!)

It wasn't until 1970 when the magnetic stripe at the back of credit cards was perfected that they became widely available. Merchants like credit cards because the issuing bank commits to pay the merchant the moment the transaction is authorized—regardless of whether or not the consumer ever pays off his or her credit card bill!

▼ Terminals "read" your card and let the merchant know it is genuine.

AUTHORIZED SIGNATURE   0000 1234

| magnetic stripe | signature of cardholder

▶ It's important to read your credit card statements to make sure they are right.

What You Need to Know

People can choose to pay the full amount they owe on their credit cards or pay a partial payment each month.

If you pay the amount of money you owe in full each month, there is usually no cost for using the credit card. However, if you cannot pay the whole credit card bill, you must pay a **finance charge**, or interest. Finance charges increase the cost of goods and services that are purchased with credit cards.

Some people make the mistake of paying only the **minimum payment** on their credit cards each month. Here's a simple way to think about it. Let's say you were paying off a loan of $200, with a 10 percent annual interest rate, by making only the minimum payment of $20 a month. Because of the added interest, it would take you about eleven months to pay off the loan and cost you an extra $10.24 in interest.

Just think if the annual percentage rate were 18 percent. You would be paying an extra $20.23 in interest. Ouch. That's a lot of interest for a $200 purchase!

▼ This girl is using a credit card to pay for her purchases.

What Are the Pros and Cons of Using Credit Cards?

Some people believe in paying cash for all purchases. Others find credit cards necessary to have and use. Credit cards have advantages and disadvantages. Much depends on how and when people use them. Credit cards may help you buy things you need or want, but you will often be paying more for what you buy. You need to think of how to best use credit cards, so consider the benefits and drawbacks before using them.

Benefits

- Convenience
- Can be used worldwide
- Buy now, enjoy your purchase, and have months or years to pay
- Good for emergencies
- Safer than cash in terms of loss, the credit card company will "stop" your card and not hold you responsible for any charges that may have been put on it by other parties
- Can buy big household necessities on credit, such as furniture or appliances
- Can receive added benefits such as frequent flyer miles or reward points

Drawbacks

- Too tempting (People often buy things they really can't afford)
- Finance charges add to the cost of goods and services—(Some finance charges are as high as 23 percent)
- If you can only afford a small monthly payment, it will take you longer to repay your debt; the longer you take, the more interest you pay

▲ Many people use credit cards to buy things they want.

Point of Information

There is no federal limit on the interest rate that credit card companies can charge! That's why it is important to shop around and compare rates.

Credit Card Smarts

Reading a Credit Card Statement

Credit card companies send monthly statements. Look at this statement to help you understand the key vocabulary terms.

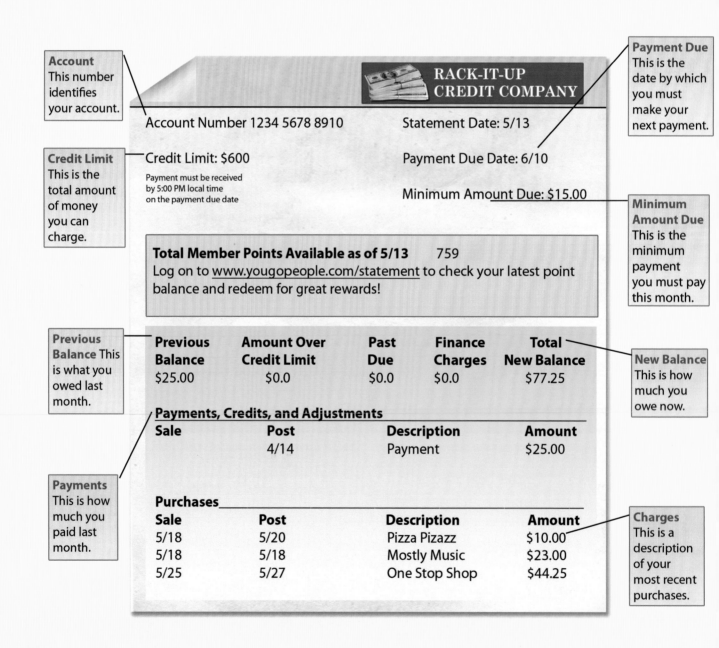

Account
This number identifies your account.

Credit Limit
This is the total amount of money you can charge.

Previous Balance This is what you owed last month.

Payments
This is how much you paid last month.

Payment Due
This is the date by which you must make your next payment.

Minimum Amount Due
This is the minimum payment you must pay this month.

New Balance
This is how much you owe now.

Charges
This is a description of your most recent purchases.

RACK-IT-UP CREDIT COMPANY

Account Number 1234 5678 8910

Statement Date: 5/13

Credit Limit: $600

Payment Due Date: 6/10

Payment must be received by 5:00 PM local time on the payment due date

Minimum Amount Due: $15.00

Total Member Points Available as of 5/13   759
Log on to www.yougopeople.com/statement to check your latest point balance and redeem for great rewards!

Previous Balance	Amount Over Credit Limit	Past Due	Finance Charges	Total New Balance
$25.00	$0.0	$0.0	$0.0	$77.25

Payments, Credits, and Adjustments

Sale	Post	Description	Amount
	4/14	Payment	$25.00

Purchases

Sale	Post	Description	Amount
5/18	5/20	Pizza Pizazz	$10.00
5/18	5/18	Mostly Music	$23.00
5/25	5/27	One Stop Shop	$44.25

Can You Avoid Credit Card Debt?

You can—if you learn to follow these five simple rules.

- Investigate loans used to finance large purchases, such as appliances and automobiles. The interest rates for these loans are generally lower than rates for credit cards.

- Think about what you give up when you purchase something with a credit card. Your future income is now reduced by the price of the item just purchased; you can't use that portion of your future income to buy anything else.

- Figure out how much you're able to pay on your credit card bill each month. When you make a purchase, be sure you'll be able to pay the bill in full at the end of the month, just like the telephone bill or any other bill.

- Lastly, before making a purchase, ask yourself: Do I really need this? Do I need it now?

Point of Information

Today we have "smart" phones. Someday soon, we'll have "smart cards." People in France are using smart cards already. These credit cards have built-in computer chips that record each transaction. So record keeping is a snap for the consumer!

"Fine for lateness."

Getting a Loan

Credit cards are only one way people borrow money. Taking out loans is another way. Who gives loans? Banks, loan agencies, and car dealerships do. Banks are the most common lenders.

Banks don't give loans to every customer who wants one. First, you have to be 18 or 21 (depending on where you live) to apply for credit. You also have to come across as someone who will pay back the loan. Bank officials will run a credit check to see how well you've managed money in the past.

▼ Families apply for loans for many things, such as homes and school.

▼ People often apply for car loans.

They want to see that you've paid bills on time. They want to know about any debt you may have.

If you've never borrowed money, the bank may require a parent or other adult to **cosign** the loan. This means that person is responsible for repaying the loan if you **default**, or don't repay the loan.

Some first-time borrowers may also need **collateral** for a loan. Collateral is personal property, such as a car, that the borrower promises to give to the lender in case of a loan default. If you don't repay the loan, the bank can sell the collateral and keep the money.

Economics in Action

Why do banks have to be careful? In recent years, most countries experienced a **recession**. A recession is when the **economy** does not grow or thrive for six months or more.

Getting a Mortgage

What's the most expensive purchase people make in their lifetimes? For most people, it's a house (or land). A **mortgage** is an agreement in which you borrow money in order to buy that house and pay back the money over a period of years. The "life" or **term** of a mortgage is long. It can be 15, 20, or 30 years!

There are different types of mortgages. Here are the four basic kinds.

- **Fixed Rate** The mortgage rate stays the same throughout the life of the mortgage. If you pay $1200 a month the first year, you still will be paying $1200 a month in the final year of the mortgage (though taxes may have gone up).

- **Adjustable Rate (ARM)** Certain rates are locked in for a period of time, such as 3, 5, 7, or 10 years. Then the rates increase to the going rate when the ARM expires.

- **Balloon Mortgage** Payments are not spread out evenly for the duration of the mortgage. Instead, the final payment is called a balloon payment because of its large size. Balloon mortgages are common for businesses but not homeowners.

- **Variable Rate** Rates are not locked in for any significant length of time. These are the riskiest kinds of mortgages. Homeowners have no way of predicting what their mortgage payments will be.

How Are Mortgage Rates Set?

Mortgage rates are different from interest rates. Who sets mortgage rates? How do they come up with the number? Mortgage lenders have control over who gets approved for a mortgage and on what terms. But they have nothing to do with mortgage rates. Mortgage rates are determined by investors, who buy the loans that lenders make.

As in the stock market, rates move up and down. When the economy is on an upswing, mortgage rates go up. In a market downturn, rates tend to drop for consumers. Experts say that the way to get the best mortgage rate is to follow financial trends and try to time your purchase accordingly.

Economics and YOU

Higher interest rates result in people saving more and borrowing less. Lower interest rates encourage people to save less and borrow more. How do you think changes in interest rates affect people's decisions to borrow in order to buy houses?

Home Sweet Home — or Not

Many factors affect mortgages. When few houses are available in an area, prices go up. When many houses become available, value and prices go down.

Still, many people dream of having a home because a home gives people their greatest **equity**. Equity is the value of something owned, such as a house, after you take away the amount of money you still owe on it. In hard times, people can get **equity loans**. They put up their homes as collateral and take out loans to pay off debt or to finance a college education.

◀ Over time, house values change.

▲ In a recession, many people lose their homes.

In recent years, many people lost their homes because they could not keep up with their monthly mortgage payments. Lenders had encouraged people to own homes by offering very low mortgage rates for a short period of time. When that period ended, people had to pay whatever the going mortgage rate was. Many could not afford the new rate, so banks had to **foreclose** by taking back people's houses when they could not repay the money they borrowed to buy them.

If you have managed your money wisely, you stand a greater chance of lowering your risk when you borrow. Riskier loans command higher interest rates than safer loans. That's because of the greater chance of the borrower defaulting on the loan—not being able to repay it. That is why there are different interest rates for individuals with good and bad **credit ratings**. Be sure you fall into the category of having a good credit rating.

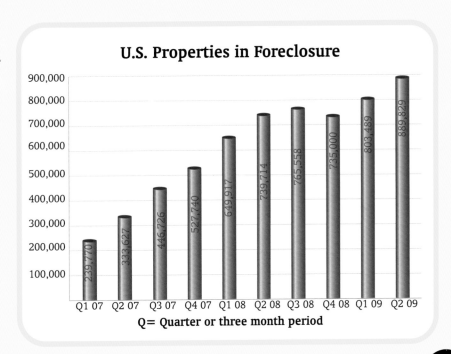

U.S. Properties in Foreclosure

Quarter	Properties
Q1 07	239,770
Q2 07	333,627
Q3 07	446,726
Q4 07	527,740
Q1 08	649,917
Q2 08	739,714
Q3 08	765,558
Q4 08	735,000
Q1 09	803,489
Q2 09	889,829

Q= Quarter or three month period

Coming to Terms

The risks of borrowing can be reduced if you approach it wisely and study the words of the agreement. Before agreeing to the terms of a loan, ask for help in figuring it out on paper. Ask for examples of the different ways you can pay back the loan.

Sometimes, you have to make difficult decisions. What can you afford to pay per month? What other monthly expenses do you have? How much do you spend on gas, for example? Do you pay for your own car insurance? How much does that cost a month?

▼ Many people borrow money to buy a car.

Suppose you've saved $1000 to use as a **down payment** on a used car. You find a car that costs $7000. The dealer is willing to give you a $6000 loan ($7000-$1000= $6000). He is offering you a loan at 5% interest for five years.

Cost: $7000
Down Payment: $1000
Amount of Loan: $6000
Terms of Loan 5 years, at 5% interest
Calculate: 5% of $6,000 is $300/year
($600 x .05 = $300)
Monthly payment: $125 ($100 plus interest)
Cost of Loan: $125/month multiplied by 60 months (5 years) = $7500
Cost of Car: At the end of 5 years, the car will have cost you $7500 ($6000 loan plus $300/year interest x 5 years)

Is this a good deal?
Yes. You'd be able to drive the car for five years while you were paying it off. The monthly payments are $125, which means you must put away or save approximately $30–$35 a week, from a part-time job.

Go Figure! Suppose the idea of a loan that lasts for five years bothers you. You want to see if you can pay it off in two years. What would you have to consider?

Total Cost: $6600 ($6000 loan, plus $300/year for 2 years interest)

Sound good? Your overall cost would be $6600, and not $7500. But what do you think that would do to your monthly payment?

Two years = 24 months
$6600 divided by 24 = $275

Your monthly payments would be $275. Yikes!

What's your final decision: Which plan suits you best?

Being Smart

How you spend your money tells a lot about you. When you are 18, you become responsible for the information that goes into a credit report. A **credit report** tells lenders how you've paid your bills in the past and whether or not you've ever filed for **bankruptcy**. Bankruptcy is when you declare you can't pay your bills. After you file for bankruptcy, you will have a hard time getting loans and credit.

Your credit rating lets lenders know how likely you are to pay back debts, based on prior experience. Having a good credit rating makes it easier to get loans and mortgages.

What's the best way to establish a good credit rating? It's never too soon to start! One way to show you are credit worthy is to get a job. If you have a job, a credit card company, for example, knows you have regular income available to pay your bills.

Another good move is to open a bank savings account and make deposits regularly. Then when you are ready to apply for credit, the savings account will show that you are a responsible money manager.

Paying bills on time is also important. Suppose you pay for your own phone. If you pay the monthly bill on time and never have to pay a late fee, you demonstrate an ability to handle money responsibly.

◀ Having a good credit report is like getting an A+ on a test.

▲ Make smart decisions when you shop.

Start Small

Once you have a job—even a part-time job—get a single credit card. Some department stores issue cards to teens, if a parent cosigns the agreement. Why is it a good idea to get a credit card? It gives you the chance to practice good spending habits. It gives a future lender the feeling that you are credit-worthy and can be trusted. It shows you are responsible when it comes to money.

Start small and think twice. Save your money when you want something—and don't buy something on credit if you don't have to. When credit cards come to you in the mail, ignore them. When stores make offers that allow you to buy items "with no payments for six months," ignore those, too. The six months will go by quickly, and you may be no more able to afford the item then.

Time To Say Good Buy!

You've learned that there are different ways to borrow money—and many reasons for borrowing. Chances are, by reading this book, you've become a smarter consumer. Pay attention to the way you manage money now. The payoff will be in your future!

Glossary

adjustable rate (ARM) When a mortgage rate is locked in for a period of time then the rate increases to the going rate

bankruptcy A situation in which you officially say that you are unable to pay your debts

balance The amount of the principal that remains after some has been paid off

balloon mortgage A mortgage that has a large final payment

borrower One who uses something that belongs to someone else

collateral A borrower's personal property, such as a car, that a lender can take if the borrower cannot repay the loan

compound interest When the interest earned in each period is added to the principal of the previous period to become the principal for the next period

consumer A person who buys goods and services

cosign To sign a document with another person, who promises to repay a loan if the borrower does not

credit Money loaned with a fee that must be repaid

credit card A card that allows consumers to buy things on credit

credit rating A judgment made by a bank or company about how likely a person is to pay his or her debts

credit report Includes information on where you live, how you pay your bills, and whether you've been sued or arrested for bankruptcy

debt Money that is owed

default When you cannot repay a loan

demand The number of consumers willing and able to purchase a good or service at a given price

down payment An initial lump sum of money in payment of a debt

economy The way money, businesses, and products are organized in a particular country

equity The value of something you own after you take away the amount of money you still owe on it

equity loan A loan acquired by putting up one's home as collateral

fee Money charged for a service

finance charge The interest you pay on a credit card bill

fixed rate When the mortgage rate stays the same throughout the life of the mortgage

foreclose To take back someone's property because the borrower cannot pay back the money borrowed to pay for it

interest Money you must pay for borrowing money

interest rate The rate, or percent, of interest that is charged on a loan

lender A person who lets someone borrow something she/he owns which she/he will get back later

loan An amount of money that is borrowed

market economy One that allows the choices people make to determine what is produced and sold

minimum payment The smallest amount of money that must be paid on a loan

mortgage An agreement to borrow money from a bank to buy a house or other property and pay back the money over a period of years

principal The amount of money that is lent to someone, to which interest is added

recession A period of time when there is less business activity than usual

simple interest Interest calculated on the original principal only; it never changes

supply The quantity of resources, goods, or services that sellers offer at various prices at a particular time

term The life of a mortgage, which can be 15, 20, or 30 years

terms The part of an agreement that specifies the conditions

variable rate When a mortgage rate is not locked in for any significant length of time

Index

Webfinder

www.themint.org/kids
http://biz.yahoo.com/pfg/e37children/
http://money.cnn.com/magazines/moneymag/money101/
www.jumpstartcoalition.org/

DATE DUE

DEMCO 38-296